P9-AGA-081

The Seagram Building

The Seagram Building

Photographs by Ezra Stoller

Introduction by Franz Schulze

building **blocks**

Princeton Architectural Press • New York

The BUILDING BLOCKS series presents the masterworks of modern architecture through the iconic images of acclaimed architectural photographer Ezra Stoller.

ADDITIONAL TITLES IN THE SERIES

The Chapel at Ronchamp
Fallingwater
The Salk Institute
Taliesin West
The TWA Terminal
The United Nations
The Yale Art + Architecture Building

Contents

Introduction

Franz Schulze

WHILE ONE OF the factors that won Mies van der Rohe the commission to design the Seagram Building was his reputation for single-mindedness verging on predictability, the solution he came up with was among the most inventive and original of his entire career. As little as a glance is required to recognize Seagram as a building by Mies, yet further study discloses features not only unique to the Miesian catalog but vital to the exceptional quality of the finished product. Furthermore, for anyone unable to visit New York, the photographs of the building by Ezra Stoller provide an unsurpassed visual record of a structure arresting unto itself and in relation to its setting. Indeed, the shot Stoller made of the building from the northwest is the one most frequently reproduced, largely because it is the most fully revealing.

In anticipation of the celebration of its one hundredth anniversary in 1958, the Joseph E. Seagram and Sons Corporation began planning as early as 1954 to put up its own building. They selected a choice piece of property in midtown Manhattan, between 52nd and 53rd streets on the east side of Park Avenue. Seagram board chairman Samuel Bronfman began the process by requesting a proposal from Luckman & Pereira, a well-regarded California firm whose design later appeared in model form in the international press. There it was seen by Bronfman's daughter Phyllis Lambert, who had some well-informed opinions of her own about the arts at large and architecture in particular. She made it clear to her father that she was monumentally unimpressed by the Luckman & Pereira design, and in a gesture as sage as it was paternal, he responded by granting her full authority over the selection of the final architect.

When Lambert called upon the Museum of Modern Art for advice, she was greeted by Philip Johnson, who at the time was about to leave his position as director of the Department of Architecture in order to give himself over wholly to his own architectural practice. Knowing that he still lacked the reputation to be a candidate for the job, Johnson proved generous in the time he gave Lambert, primarily because he recognized that Seagram's plan to hire the best possible architect and treat him to a lavish budget would to some degree offset the sorry abundance of second rate building in New York in the boom of the mid-1950s.

Working together, Lambert and Johnson nominated close to a dozen renowned designers, including Eero Saarinen, Marcel Breuer, and I. M. Pei. They narrowed the field to Frank Lloyd Wright, Le Corbusier, and Mies, then to the latter two, and finally to Mies himself. Lambert later justified the choice, observing that "the younger men, the second generation, are talking in terms of Mies,"[1] but a measure of the Seagram decision to award him the commission derived from the suspicion that both Le Corbusier and Wright would have proven temperamentally too difficult to work with. Mies, by contrast, was the least likely to force his ego on the project—in short, the most trustworthy, the most predictable.

In retrospect, then, his solution could be readily imagined from the start, and in the most obvious visible respects, it lived up to that expectation. From the street the Seagram Building appears as a tall, rectangular prism, perceptibly related to the apartment towers Mies erected earlier in the 1950s on Chicago's Lake Shore Drive. Those buildings had earned him much of the publicity that led finally to the Seagram commission. They were studies in a clear, straightforward, typically Miesian relationship of steel frame and glass infill. The structure and the skin occupied the same plane, and, by applying I-beams to all exposed vertical members, Mies achieved a nearly regular *a-b-b-b-a* rhythm of column and mullion. The I-beams also added a lean but persuasive decorative element to the facade.

The Seagram Building, executed when central air conditioning was more readily available, called for a vent situated between the structural columns and the outer glass skin. As a consequence the skin was separated from the structure, and the rhythm of the exterior vertical members making up the curtain wall became exactly regular in its expression.

All of the above, while descriptive of the surfaces of the Chicago towers and their later derivation at Seagram's, leaves untouched a substantial amount of what lies at the heart of Mies's achievement in both places. While critics have often accused him of indifference to the surroundings of his buildings, in both the Chicago and New York instances, that criticism has little merit. The relationship of the two apartment buildings to each other and to the Lake Michigan

860–880 Lake Shore Drive, Chicago, 1958–51.

shoreline is one of the most winning aspects of that design, and in New York Mies's response to the context of the Seagram Building is even more impressive.

Among the earliest of his self-imposed duties was a careful, characteristically deliberate study of the area adjacent to the chosen site. There he found the buildings facing Park Avenue built consistently close to the sidewalk and in deference to local zoning laws. Regulations prohibited any building to rise above a certain height without the progressive setbacks that caused so many Manhattan highrises to be capped by ziggurat-like masses. Since such a shape was unacceptable to Mies, who constitutionally preferred simpler forms, he chose to turn much of the site into a plaza extending from 52nd to 53rd streets and to set his building in the form of a severely polyhedral slab one hundred feet behind it. As Lambert wrote,

> . . . he has a cardboard model made of Park Avenue between 46th and 57th streets with all the buildings on the Avenue and some going in the blocks and then he has a number of towers for different solutions that he places in the empty place of the old 375 [the Park Avenue address] and this model is up on a high table so that when sitting in a chair his eye is just level with the table top which equals the street—and for hours on end he peers down his Park Avenue trying out the different towers.[2]

Among the ideas Mies considered for the tower were one square in plan and another in rectangular slab form that would have been set perpendicular to the avenue. Both of these he discarded in favor of a third possibility, borne out in the structure that now stands parallel to the street. Its thirty-nine stories ascended to a height of 516 feet, the loftiest of any high rise he ever completed. So conceived, it proved a canny way of bowing to the zoning laws while opening up a space that was at the time unprecedented on Park Avenue, and ample enough to enable the viewer to comprehend the building equally well from both sides of the avenue.

Even so, despite the building's height and size, the design had sacrificed a significant amount of floor space to accommodate the plaza. Mies then devised a deftly inventive way of providing that space while remaining true to most (though as we will see, not all) of his customary habits. To the rear of the slab he attached a one-bay-deep "spine" that rose the full thirty-nine stories, and added to it a three-bay-deep, ten-story-high "bustle" flanked in turn by two three-bay-deep, four-story-high wings. Thus he managed to add an enormous amount of floor area to what had become a complicated overall form, without surrendering the splendid simplicity of the main slab, which remains the dominant element of the building.

At the same time, it is worth noting that he took several other approaches uncommon in his work both earlier and later. He had never designed so compartmentalized a high rise before, nor had he ever secured any tall structure against the horizontal force of the wind by the use of shear walls that, in this case, rose on the north and south sides of the spine. In yet another atypical gesture, he clad these walls with Tinian marble, superimposing on their surfaces the same curtain wall elements that made up the rest of the facade.

ANYONE WHO examines the completed building from the avenue or the side streets cannot help observing the stern symmetry of the design, which confirms Mies's well-known reputation as a modernist in style but a classicist in principle. The facade, precise in its

The Seagram Building viewed from the north, revealing the "bustle" to the rear of the Park Avenue facade. This addition provided desired floorspace without compromising the simplicity of the overall form.

View to the west from the lobby of the Seagram Building, showing the Racquet and Tennis Cub across Park Avenue, by McKim, Mead & White, 1918.

detailing and affectingly certain in its proportions, is five bays wide, with the canopied entrance located directly between the third and fourth piers. The striation of all the columns can be read as an abstract form of fluting, and the three steps leading from the sidewalk to the plaza act as a modernist adaptation of the classical temple stereobate. The plaza itself, covered in pink granite, features two shallow rectangular pools, identical in dimensions and situated at the far corners. Directly next to the outer edge of each basin is a Tinian marble bench that, on the one hand, reflects the sobriety of Mies's manner, and, on the other, says more than a little about the sociability of New Yorkers, who flock to the benches in the summertime, turning the space into a kind of outdoor conversation pit.

From that very place on the plaza, a view to the west discloses another happy aspect of the success of the total design package. On the other side of Park Avenue parallel with the facade of the Seagram Building is the Racquet and Tennis Club, a neo-Florentine palazzo erected in 1918 by the storied firm of McKim, Mead & White. The differences between the two buildings consist of more than a chronology of forty years. The older structure is a solid piece of masonry historicist in style; the newer by contrast is open, vitreous and equally assured in its modernist abstraction. Yet they are joined by an underlying commitment to classicism that suggests a happy marriage of opposites.

ANY CONSIDERATION of the treatment of the interior spaces must return Philip Johnson to the narrative. After Mies appointed the office of Kahn & Jacobs of New York as his associate architects, he took it upon himself to invite Johnson to serve as his partner in the project. The idea had manifold merit. As a departmental head at the

Museum of Modern Art, Johnson was already a figure of consequence in the American architectural world, and the few buildings he had designed on his own marked him as a devoted Miesian disciple. Thus the value of his assistance to Mies in advancing work on the Seagram Building speaks for itself. Furthermore, by issuing the invitation, Mies was in an ideal position to repay Johnson for the many favors the latter had done him, dating back to Mies's days in Germany, when Johnson played a crucial role in bringing his work to the attention of an American public.

In virtually all significant respects Johnson proved equal to his tasks. Only one of his proposals failed to find favor with Mies. He had suggested that the whole plaza consist of a pool of water, to be contained by a marble wall, with a footbridge providing access from Park Avenue to the main entrance. Mies didn't reject it so much as he ignored it, and the plaza as finally constructed is his alone. Otherwise, however, Johnson fulfilled his assignments handsomely. He was responsible for the design of the elevators, the lighting throughout the building, and the glass canopies that cover the entrance pathways leading to the building from 52nd and 53rd streets. Even more notable, however, were his plans for furnishing the two commodious rooms in the wings extending outward from the bustle. These spaces followed Mies's design, but it was Johnson who equipped them with a pair of bar-restaurants that have remained among New York's elite watering places ever since the Seagram Building opened to the public in 1959. In the northern room Johnson achieved a variation of his plan for an aqueous plaza by surrounding a walled pool with tables and classic Mies-designed chairs, which form a striking and elegant ensemble. The space in the southern wing also houses a refectory, simpler in decor but comparably handsome. It is here that Johnson, now well into his nineties, has regularly entertained guests at his private table. It was also Johnson who early on helped to acquire the Picasso tapestry that hangs on a wall between the entrances to the restaurants.

What remains to be cited in this discussion is Mies's use of materials, a factor of perpetual importance to him in all his work. The generous budget provided him at Seagram enabled him to treat all the passages within and without the structure with exceptional refinement. The plaza is paved in a high grade pink granite. The foyer features four ranks of elevators clad in quality travertine, and the soffit above them is lined with glass mosaic in pinkish-gray, a color akin to that used in all the windows. But the material most responsible for the understated opulence of the Seagram Building as a whole is the bronze of the curtain wall, a substance whose warmth is matched by its connotations of historic age. Mies's own respect for the material, not to mention his authority over it, is evident from the treatment to which he subjected the exterior vertical I-beams, by the mid-1950s a standard part of the Miesian constructive vocabulary. Johnson himself forever marveled at Mies's determination to widen the edge of the flange, just enough to keep it from looking insubstantial, but executed subtly enough to escape all but the most scrupulous notice.

VAST PUBLICITY attended the Seagram Building in the course of its construction and continued once it was finished—on a note of irony. The New York Tax Commission decided to impose a tax on the building roughly 50% higher than that applicable to a more inexpensive structure. The Commission claimed that the Seagram company had spent a substantial amount for the value of prestige, and prestige was regarded as taxable. The outcry against the ruling was summed up in the headline "Legislating Against Quality," an article in the May 26, 1963 issue of *The New York Times* by critic Ada Louise Huxtable. The Seagram company took the case to court and lost.

In a sense, however, the contest did not end there. In fact, as time passes, it becomes ever more apparent that the real winners were the company and, above all, the architect. The decision to grant the commission to Mies van der Rohe and award him the kind of budget he was uniquely able to exploit has left New York, America, and the world in possession of a work of art that qualifies at the end of the millennium for the title of the best skyscraper ever built.

NOTES

1. Phyllis Lambert, "How a Building Gets Built," *Vassar Alumnae Magazine* (February 1959): 13.

2. Lambert, Letter to Eve Borsook, 1 December 1954, quoted in "How a Building Gets Built," p. 17.

Plates

2-10

NO SMOKING

Drawings & Plans

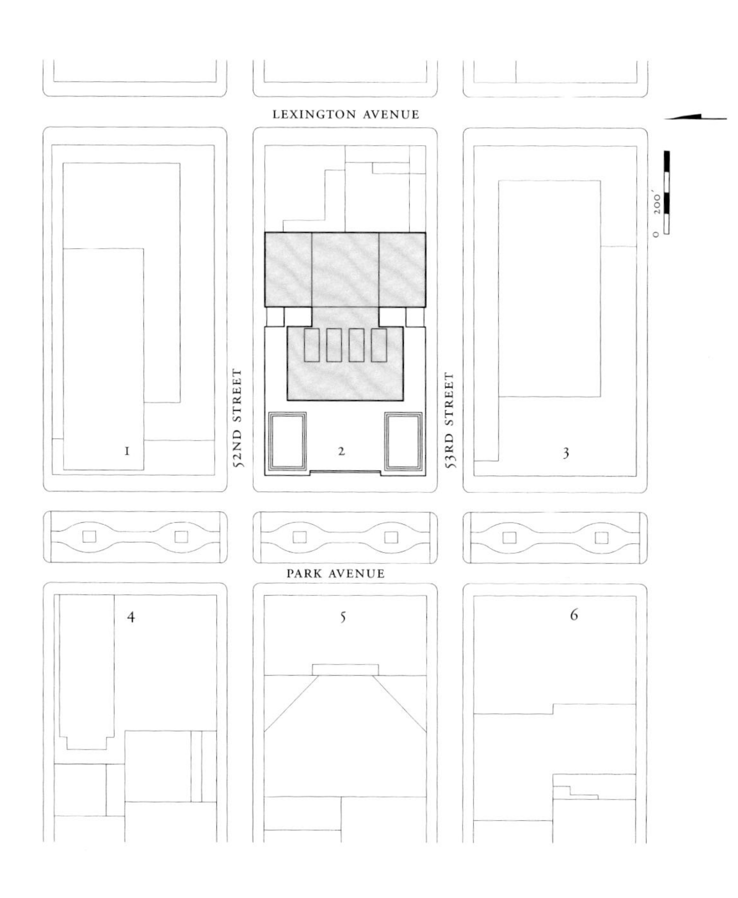

1. FIRST NATIONAL CITY BANK (399 PARK AVE.)

2. SEAGRAM BUILDING, 1958

3. 345 PARK AVE.

4. LEVER HOUSE (390 PARK AVE), SKIDMORE, OWINGS & MERRIL, 1950–52

5. RACQUET AND TENNIS CLUB (370 PARK AVE), MCKIM, MEAD & WHITE, 1918

6. MANUFACTURERS HANOVER BANK BUILDING (350 PARK AVE.)

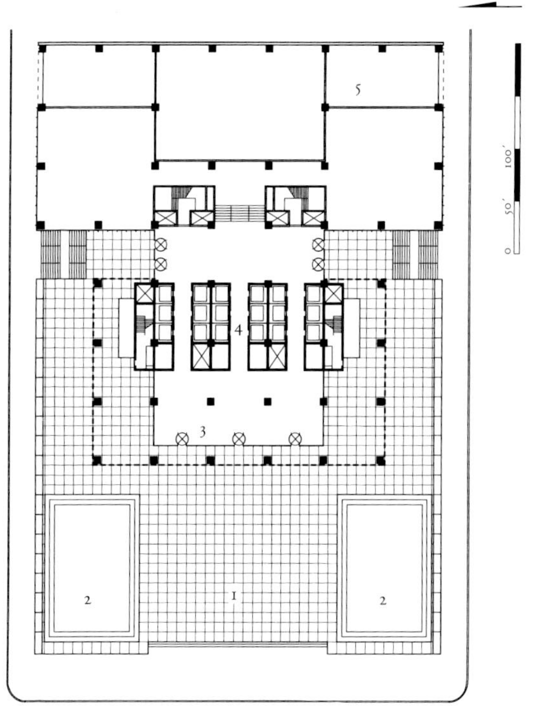

PARK AVENUE

1. PLAZA
2. FOUNTAIN
3. LOBBY
4. ELEVATORS
5. DINING

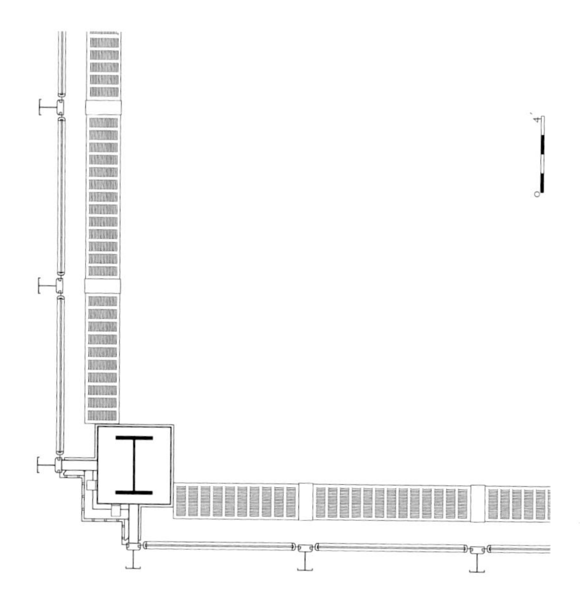

CORNER DETAIL

Key to Photographs

Published by
Princeton Architectural Press
37 East Seventh Street
New York, NY 10003

For a catalog of books published by Princeton Architectural Press, call toll free 800.722.6657
or visit www.papress.com

10 09 08 07 06   5 4 3 2   First Edition

Series editor: Mark Lamster
Project editor: Therese Kelly
Book design: Mark Lamster and Therese Kelly
Drawings & plans: Dan Herman and Linda Chung

Acknowledgments
On behalf of my father, I would like to thank my colleagues at Esto Photographics,
especially Kent Draper and Laura Bolli; Mary Doyle and Mike Kimines of TSI Color Lab
for their help in preparing these images; and Mark Lamster for his support from start to
finish.—Erica Stoller

Princeton Architectural Press acknowledges Ann Alter, Eugenia Bell, Jan Cigliano, Jane
Garvie, Caroline Green, Beth Harrison, Clare Jacobson, Mirjana Javornik, Leslie Ann Kent,
Sara Moss, Anne Nitschke, Lottchen Shivers, Sara E. Stemen, and Jennifer Thompson
—Kevin C. Lippert, publisher

For the licensing of Ezra Stoller images, contact Esto Photographics.

Printed in China

Library of Congress Cataloging-in-Publication Data

The Seagram Building / photographs by Ezra Stoller; introduction by Franz Schulze.
p. cm. -- (Building Blocks)
Includes bibliographical references.
ISBN 1-56898-201-1 (alk. paper)
1. Seagram Building (New York, N.Y.) Pictorial works. 2. Architecture, Modern—20th century
—New York (State)—New York Pictorial works. 3. New York (N.Y.)—Buildings, structures, etc
Pictorial works. 3. Mies van der Rohe, Ludwig, 1886–1969—Criticism and interpretation.
I. Stoller, Ezra. II. Series: Building blocks series (New York, N.Y.)
NA6233.N5 S437 1999
725′ .2′097471--dc21   99-35127
CIP